STA/CH

Collins Care for your
Puppy

RSPCA
PET GUIDE

Contents

D0995426

New 3rd Edition
First published in 2004 by
Collins, an imprint of
HarperCollins*Publishers*
77-85 Fulham Palace Road
Hammersmith
London W6 8JB

The Collins website is www.collins.co.uk

Collins is a registered trademark of HarperCollins Publishers Limited

14 13 12 11 10
20 19 18

First published as *Care for your Puppy* in 1985 by
William Collins Sons & Co Ltd, London

Second edition published in 1990

Reprinted by HarperCollins*Publishers*
and subsequently reprinted 12 times

The RSPCA is a registered charity (no. 219099)
The RSPCA website is www.rspca.org.uk

Designed by: SP Creative Design
Editor: Heather Thomas
Design: Rolando Ugolini

Front jacket picture: © Getty Images Photodisc

Photographs:
Angela Hampton/RSPCA Photolibrary: page 25
Cheryl Ertelt/RSPCA Photolibrary: pages 26 & 27

A catalogue record for this book is available from the British Library

ISBN-13 978 0 00 718268 8

Colour reproduction by Saxon Photolitho, Norfolk
Printed and bound by Printing Express Ltd, Hong Kong

Foreword

Owning a dog is great fun but a huge responsibility. All pets need a regular routine and lots of love and attention. But, most importantly, pet dogs need owners who are going to stay interested in them and will be committed to them all their lives.

Anyone who has ever enjoyed the company of a dog knows just how strong the bond can be. Children learn the meaning of loyalty, unselfishness and friendship by growing up with animals. Elderly or lonely people often depend on a pet for company and it has been proved that animals can help in the prevention of and recovery from physical or mental illness.

The decision to bring a puppy into your home should always be discussed and agreed by everyone in the family. Bear in mind that parents are ultimately responsible for the health and well-being of the animal for the whole of its lifetime. If you are not prepared for the inevitable expense, time, patience and occasional frustration involved, then the RSPCA would much rather that you didn't have a dog.

Being responsible for a dog will completely change your life but if you make the decision to go ahead, think about offering a home to one of the thousands of animals in RSPCA animal centres throughout England and Wales. No animals are more deserving of loving owners.

As for the care of your pet, this book should provide you with all the information you need to know to keep it happy and healthy for many years to come. Enjoy the experience!

Steve Cheetham MA,
Vet MB, MRCVS
Chief Veterinary Officer,
RSPCA

Introduction

Before you commit yourself to a puppy, think carefully about whether you can afford to keep a dog, whether your home is suitable, and whether dog ownership will fit into your lifestyle.

● **Keeping a dog is quite costly**. Apart from the obvious initial expenses of dog ownership, such as the purchase price and cost of housing and accessories, there is the mounting cost of feeding as the puppy grows bigger. Insurance can help cover the cost of veterinary care which is sure to be needed from time to time, but even vaccinations can be expensive. You must also be prepared for the cost of boarding kennels when you go on holiday.

● **Dogs need space**. When you consider whether your house and garden are large enough, remember that many small puppies grow into larger dogs. Sadly, many of the larger breeds are abandoned or have to be rehomed when the owners discover that their homes are too small. Make sure you know what size your puppy will grow to, how much space it will need and how much it will eat.

▼ Cross-breds or mongrels? These eight-week-old puppies suggest possible German Shepherd and Labrador ancestry.

● **Dogs need company**. They are pack animals by instinct and are unhappy if they are left too much on their own. Therefore, you should not take on the commitment of owning a puppy unless someone will be at home most of the time to look after it. You must also be prepared to devote some of your time each day to exercising, training and grooming your puppy. It will grow up to regard you, its owner, as its pack leader and will expect to take part in the life of your family.

● **Are you very house-proud?** If so, you may not be prepared to tolerate the inevitable stains and smells associated with a small puppy, possible damage to furniture and furnishings and unavoidable dog hairs.

● **Can you offer stability?** Many dogs suffer stress as a result of the arrival of a new spouse or a new baby, or removal to another new home. It is best to delay buying a puppy until you can offer it stability during the first few months of its life.

Pedigree or mongrel?

A large proportion of puppies are born as a result of accidental or casually arranged matings. Puppies of unplanned pregnancies are usually cross-breds or mongrels and tend, for genetic reasons, to be physically more robust and temperamentally more stable than some inbred pedigree puppies.

◄ Among pedigree dogs, the Cocker Spaniel is a popular choice. It is a good companion, but it can be difficult with young children. Its appetite for exercise and play is enormous.

Pedigree puppies

Pedigree puppies have parents of the same recognized breed. They are certainly the most expensive but may not necessarily be the 'best buy'. Some puppies suffer from over-breeding, resulting in genetic weaknesses and sometimes difficulties of temperament. Against this, most breeds have largely consistent patterns of behaviour so that the owner knows what to expect of the grown dog. Pedigree puppies should be bought from a recognized breeder and should have been registered with The Kennel Club.

Cross-bred puppies

Cross-breds are the puppies born to pure-bred parents of different breeds. The puppies will inherit half their genes from their mother and half from their father. As the genes control all the myriad characteristics of size, shape, colour, coat type, and so on, as well as intelligence and temperamental traits, the resulting puppies will show a combination of both parents' looks and temperaments, and can be highly attractive.

Mongrel puppies

Mongrel puppies are those of mixed ancestry and no definable breed. When breeding pedigree puppies, the choice of parents (and therefore of genetic material) is strictly limited; with the mongrel population the choice is unlimited. This accounts for the diversity, strength and hardiness of mongrel puppies, and for their relative lack of inherited and congenital disorders. They can make delightful pets.

The RSPCA and other animal welfare organizations are good sources of healthy mongrels and cross-breds.

Which sex?

Personal taste apart, there is very little significance in the choice between a male and a female puppy. Traditionally, bitches are thought to be more home-loving and dogs more aggressive, but if, as recommended, the puppies are neutered these distinctions largely disappear.

Females

Most female puppies can be expected to reach puberty at some time between six and twelve months, when they will normally have their first oestrus or season (they 'come on heat'). For the rest of their life they will then season every six to twelve months, each one lasting for about three weeks, during which time the male dogs over a wide area will be attracted by the bitch's scent. In the first few days of the season there are discharges of mucus and blood which can stain furniture and carpets. Bitches in season constantly clean themselves and may show changes in temperament, such as unnatural lethargy or excitability.

▲ Puppies should always stay with their mother until they are at least eight weeks old.

For these reasons, but mostly because of the high risk of pregnancy, most owners will seek to control their pet's oestrus. Some will pen up the bitch or even board her at their local kennels during this time; some will attempt control by using special deodorant sprays; others will use prescribed hormonal treatment from their vet. However, the most satisfactory means of control, from the point of view of both the bitch and its owner, is spaying (see opposite).

Males

A male puppy can be expected to reach maturity at between eight and twelve months, by which time he will be displaying characteristic dog behaviour. This may include roaming in search of bitches, and aggression with other dogs or with people. He will also spray urine to mark his territory. Such behaviour can be worrying, dangerous and embarrassing for the owner. Unlike the female, the male dog is sexually active throughout the year.

A male dog's sexual behaviour can be controlled medicinally, but many owners prefer to have their dog castrated by a veterinary surgeon (see opposite). Ask your vet for advice on how you should proceed with your dog.

Neutering

The abandonment of thousands of unwanted puppies each year is one of the tragedies of modern society. Unless it is intended to breed seriously from a puppy and the owner can guarantee good homes for all the offspring, a pet dog should be neutered.

▲ Exploration and play are the mainsprings of puppies' lives. These are between eleven and twelve weeks old.

What age to neuter?
Veterinary surgeons have differing views on the best age for neutering a dog but, bearing in mind that some bitches reach puberty at six months and some dogs at eight months, new owners of puppies should not delay long before taking veterinary advice. Generally, bitches should be spayed before their first season, to avoid any risk of pregnancy, and males between seven and twelve months.

Complications and risks
Both spaying and castration are carried out under general anaesthetic. The operations are simple, complications are rare and recovery is swift. Certainly the risks of spaying to a bitch are less than the risks associated with pregnancy and birth.

Advantages of neutering
Unneutered males will be attracted by bitches on heat in their locality, and will follow them if they get the opportunity. This can not only lead to dog-fights, traffic accidents and the worrying of farm livestock but also, at best, anxiety for the owner when their dog goes missing.

If they are unable to mate, male dogs may simulate intercourse with a chair or a visitor's leg. Unneutered bitches on heat will attract attention from dogs and must, in effect, be confined under close house arrest until their season is over. They are also prone to phantom pregnancies which will need veterinary treatment. Sexual frustration frequently results in over-excitement in bitches and aggression in dogs.

It is a commonly held belief that neutering may cause a dog to become overweight. This is untrue, but a neutered animal may well need less food than before. Veterinary advice should be taken on this. As neutering is normally carried out at the time of change from puppy rations to an adult diet (see pages 20–22), it is not difficult to make the appropriate adjustments to your dog's feeding regime.

Size

Dogs vary in size more than any other pet animal. In height they range from the Irish Wolfhound, standing 81 cm (32 in) at the shoulder, down to the Yorkshire Terrier, standing only 20 cm (8 in) high.

The weight range is just as great. The Chihuahua weighs perhaps 1 kg (2 lb), the St Bernard 70 kg (150 lb), and mongrels can be as heavy as 36 kg (80 lb). Size, then, is an important consideration which is all too often ignored when choosing a dog. For some reason, people will not accept how much small puppies can grow.

Giant Breeds
36–84 kg (80–185 lb)

Bloodhounds
Deerhounds
Great Danes (illustrated)
Mastiffs and Bull Mastiffs
Newfoundlands
Pyrenean Mountain Dogs
St Bernards
Irish Wolfhounds

Large Breeds
23–36 kg (50–80 lb)

Afghan Hounds
Borzois
Dobermanns
German Shepherd Dogs
(illustrated)
Giant Schnauzers
Greyhounds
Irish Setters
Old English Sheepdogs
Rhodesian Ridgebacks
Rottweilers
Salukis
Weimaraners

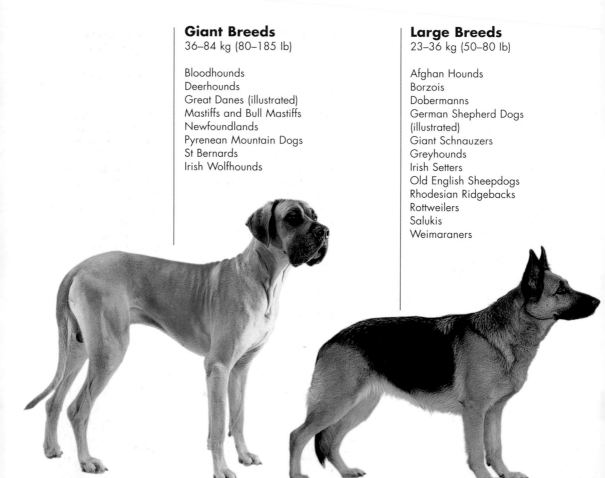

Which size is best?

For ordinary family life, dogs from the small and middle ranges are best. Most are physically robust and will fit with reasonable comfort into a family-sized house and car, enabling them to accompany their owners on most outings. As a general rule, the large breeds are remarkably tolerant of children and are good guard dogs too, but they do need much more space and more food.

The size of a breed is not necessarily a good guide to its lifestyle. For example, all spaniels are essentially outdoor dogs and need a good deal of daily exercise. The Dalmatian, although classed as a medium breed like the Spaniels, needs rather less exercise but will often find itself family duties such as guarding children. It is important to choose a puppy whose lifestyle, as an adult, will match your own.

Medium Breeds
13.5–23 kg (30–50 lb)

Basset Hounds
Boxers
Bulldogs
Chow Chows
Collies, Bearded Collies, and Border Collies
Dalmatians
Keeshonds
Pointers and German Pointers
Poodles (Standard),
Retrievers (including Labradors)
Samoyeds
Spaniels (Clumber, Field, English (illustrated) and Welsh Springer, Sussex, Irish Water)
Terriers (Airedale, Irish, Kerry Blue, Soft-Coated Wheaten)

Small Breeds
4.5 13.5 kg (10–30 lb)

Basenjis
Beagles
Bull Terriers, and Staffordshire Bull Terriers
Dachshunds
French Bulldogs
Poodles (Miniature)
Schipperkes
Schnauzers and Miniature Schnauzers
Shetland Sheepdogs
Shih Tzu
Spaniels (Cocker and American Cocker)
Terriers (except those listed as medium or toy) (West Highland White illustrated)
Welsh Corgis
Whippets

Toy Breeds
1–4.5 kg (2–10 lb)

Cavalier King Charles Spaniels
Chihuahuas
English Toy Terriers
Griffons Bruxsellois
Italian Greyhounds
Japanese Chin
King Charles Spaniels
Maltese Miniature Pinschers
Papillons
Pekingese
Pomeranians (illustrated)
Pugs
Silky Terriers
Yorkshire Terriers

Breed types

Not all pedigree puppies will grow up into suitable family pets. This is because each breed was originally evolved to fulfil a specific purpose for which its inherent qualities of speed, size, stamina, conformation and temperament are well suited.

Hounds

Hounds were bred to hunt other animals (as shown below in brackets), either by sight or by scent. Examples of sight hounds are the Afghan Hound (leopard), Borzoi (wolf), Greyhound (hare and deer), Irish Wolfhound (wolf), Rhodesian Ridgeback (lion) and Saluki (gazelle). All these dogs are long-legged and swift. Scent hounds, by contrast, are short-legged and are well adapted to follow a trail by scent. They include the Basset Hound, Beagle and Bloodhound. Hounds have both the instinct and stamina to range wide over the countryside.

▲ Irish Wolfhound

Terriers

These are the smallest of the hunting breeds. They take their name from the Latin word *terra*, meaning earth, for they work by going to earth themselves to bolt their quarry. As so many of the breed names suggest – Airedale, Border, Irish, Kerry Blue, Lakeland, Scottish, Skye, Welsh, West Highland, etc. – terriers were kept on large estates and farms to control vermin, badgers, foxes and otters.

▲ Border Terrier

By nature tough, energetic, loyal and fearless, those terriers that adapt to pet life are valued as lively companions and reliable house dogs, but they may be aggressive with strangers.

▼ Labrador Retriever

Gundogs

These breeds are trained to assist us in finding, pointing and retrieving game birds and waterfowl, whether from land or from water. Because their traditional role is not to kill but to co-operate, they are obedient, biddable and dependable. The gundogs include Setters, Pointers, Retrievers and Spaniels. Of these, the Golden Retriever and Labrador Retriever probably adapt to life as a pet dog better than any other sporting breeds, but their superb natures should not be abused by lack of exercise.

Working dogs

These include the breeds trained to herd sheep and cattle, such as the Collie, German Shepherd Dog, Old English Sheepdog and Welsh Corgi; those bred to guard people, property and animals, such as the Boxer, Bull Mastiff, Dobermann, Great Dane and Rottweiler; those polar breeds that are used for drawing sleighs, including the Alaskan Malamute, Samoyed and Siberian Husky; and the two famous rescue breeds, the St Bernard and the Newfoundland. All are country dogs and must not be kept too confined. Response to training and the need for very active lives are characteristics in all working breeds. No one should consider the ownership of a working dog unless it can be guaranteed very strict and comprehensive training, including obedience training, plenty of exercise and a lifestyle in which it can use or sublimate its working potential. If not, difficulties and frustration for both the owner and dog are inevitable.

▲ Dobermann

Utility dogs

Utility dogs are those breeds that are not included in the sporting or working categories above, yet which were once bred for a particular role, although most are now successfully kept as pets. Notable members of this group include the Bulldog (bred originally for bull-baiting), Chow Chow (bred for its fur and meat in the East), Dalmatian (a carriage escort dog), Keeshond (a Dutch barge dog), Poodle (a performing dog bred from a water retriever) and Shih Tzu (the lion dog of China).

Toy dogs

These include miniature versions of the larger breeds and have been bred as lapdogs or for the show bench. They are inexpensive to feed, need little exercise and have many devotees among those who like a constant companion about the house. However, selective breeding for small size has rendered them, as a group, delicate and rather excitable. Well-known toy breeds are the Chihuahua, Maltese, Papillon, Pekingese, Pomeranian, Pug and Yorkshire Terrier.

▲ Chow Chow

Note: Not only the toy breeds suffer hereditary defects. Centuries of inbreeding have weakened many breeds, making them prone to such defects as cataracts, deafness, haemophilia, elongated soft palates, epilepsy, hip dysplasia, hernias, progressive retinal atrophy and many more. Early veterinary examination is recommended.

▼ Yorkshire Terrier puppies

Biology

Stance The Labrador Retriever illustrates an example of good stance, but selective breeding has produced many variations, which can predispose to certain disorders.

The hind limbs The crouching stance of the German Shepherd Dog is achieved because its hind limbs are in permanent flexion, resulting in a sloping spine and exacerbating the possibility of posterior paralysis and hip dysplasia. In contrast, the overextension of the hind limbs of taller dogs, such as Great Danes and Newfoundlands, can cause the stifle joint to dislocate backwards.

The fore limbs The enormous width of the chest of the Bulldog can cause the fore limbs to bow, resulting in uneven wear on the joints. Long-backed, short-legged breeds, such as Dachshunds, may also have bowed fore limbs and splayed-out toes. Both problems can result in arthritis.

Head and eyes Selective breeding has resulted in variations ranging from the elongated eyes of the long-nosed dogs, such as the Greyhound and Collie, to the protuberant eyes of short-faced breeds, such as the Pug and Pekingese.

In general, the long-nosed dogs suffer fewer disadvantages than the short-faced breeds. The short-nosed dogs can suffer breathing difficulties, overcrowded teeth, and eczema in the folds of the skin. The protuberant eyes, just by their prominence, are predisposed to irritation and accidental damage that may give rise to corneal ulcers. They also flatten and distort the tear ducts so tears tend to run down the cheeks.

Genitalia In an increasing number of male pedigree puppies, the testicles do not descend into the scrotal sac normally. At the time of purchase, it may be found that the puppy has only one testicle in the scrotum – or even none. This is usually a hereditary defect, and it is reprehensible in law to sell such a puppy without drawing attention to the condition.

The undescended testicle can sometimes be located in the groin. If not, then it is inside the abdominal cavity. Sometimes it will descend at a later date, but if after six months this has not occurred, it is not likely to do so. Unfortunately, such a condition can lead to serious problems from middle age onwards.

Ears A puppy with erect ears is less likely to suffer ear trouble than one with folded ears. Folded ears prevent good ventilation of the ear canal not only by obstructing its entrance, but also by distorting the canal further by their sheer weight.

Debris, such as dust, grit, grass seeds and wax, accumulates and becomes trapped in a folded ear, predisposing it to infections caused by anaerobic bacteria which thrive in such an environment.

Woolly-coated dogs, such as Poodles, which do not moult, need to have the hair in the ear canal plucked to increase the circulation of air and also to prevent the accumulation of debris.

Ear cropping is one mutilation that is thankfully not carried out in the UK, but in certain European countries, for example, some breeds may still have their ears cropped (i.e. cut) to 'improve' their outline.

Teething Some puppies have trouble teething. They may have a gum infection or, more often, sore gums and persistent milk teeth. Gum infections will need veterinary treatment, but chewing on a large marrow bone, or a manufactured dog chew, will help to relieve soreness and complete shedding of the milk teeth.

If the deciduous canines are not shed in time, it may be necessary to have them extracted. If not, they can either cause the permanent canines to be displaced, or cause them to decay as a result of food being trapped between the persistent milk canines and the newly erupting permanent teeth.

Permanent teeth A full set of permanent teeth comprises, in the upper jaw: 3 incisors at the front, then 1 canine, 4 premolars and 2 molars on each side and in the lower jaw, 3 incisors, 1 canine, 4 premolars, and 3 molars on each side. This gives a total of 42 teeth.

There is considerable variation, but in general big dogs teethe before the toy breeds. Between two and five months of age, the permanent upper front incisors erupt, then the lower incisors, followed by the premolars. The canines are usually through by the age of six months. Last to appear are the permanent molars, but even these are in place and dentition is complete by the age of eight months.

Tail docking Traditionally, certain breeds of dogs, such as the Pembroke Welsh Corgi and the Old English Sheepdog, have had their tails docked. The purpose of this has been largely cosmetic. Tail docking has become an increasingly contentious issue in recent years, and it is banned in many countries. In Britain, the RSPCA has campaigned against the practice for many years.

Claws A puppy's nails should not be clipped while it is very young. Once allowed out, after vaccination (see page 36), the puppy will usually wear down its own claws naturally by exercising on hard ground and pavements. If clipped before this, there is a tendency for the claws to lose their curvature and grow straight.

Split and fractured claws, damaged by the exuberant play of puppies, can cause bleeding and tenderness, and sometimes infection of the nail-bed, all of which need veterinary attention.

Dew claws Puppies are born with dew claws on the fore limbs, and 20–30 per cent also have dew claws on the hind limbs. The front ones seldom give trouble, but the hind ones tend to get torn and may bleed profusely.

Although any mutilation is questionable on ethical grounds, many veterinary surgeons feel that, to avoid trauma, it is preferable to remove the hind dew claws at the age of 3–5 days. There are certain exceptions. For instance, the breed standard for Pyrenean Mountain Dogs requires that the hind dew claws should be retained.

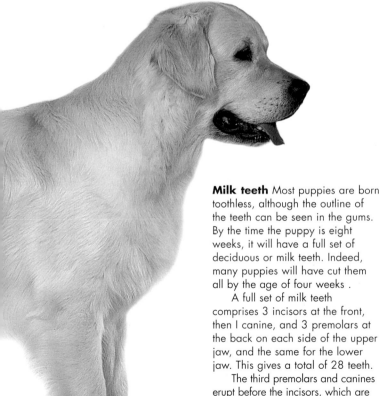

Milk teeth Most puppies are born toothless, although the outline of the teeth can be seen in the gums. By the time the puppy is eight weeks, it will have a full set of deciduous or milk teeth. Indeed, many puppies will have cut them all by the age of four weeks .

A full set of milk teeth comprises 3 incisors at the front, then I canine, and 3 premolars at the back on each side of the upper jaw, and the same for the lower jaw. This gives a total of 28 teeth.

The third premolars and canines erupt before the incisors, which are cut in succession (from the sides towards the centre of the mouth), and those in the upper jaw appear before those in the lower jaw. The first and second premolars are the last to erupt. Puppies lose their deciduous teeth between two and six months.

Housing

The need for privacy

Every puppy should be allocated a place of its own where it can be territorial and have some privacy away from the family. Fortunate puppies will have one place in the house and a kennel or outhouse in the garden. If a puppy is to grow up with a happy lack of neurotic behaviour traits, such as chewing its own paws, and howling and barking when alone, this privacy is of paramount importance. No puppy should be left alone all day while the family is out, but quiet periods alone are beneficial. The family must accept this fact and avoid disturbing and overstimulating the puppy just because it is new and appealing.

In the house it is difficult to find a place that is exclusively the puppy's domain, but the puppy's bed must be positioned in a relatively undisturbed place, free of draughts but also away from any direct source of heat. Sometimes a conservatory is suitable, but beware of overheating in summer when a glazed roof can concentrate the heat of the sun.

Playpens

Many owners find it very convenient to use a playpen to contain a young puppy at night and for periods during the day. A child's playpen can be adapted with the addition of wire-mesh or weld mesh, and, for as long as it contains the puppy safely, the playpen can be used outdoors in the garden or inside the house.

▼ When you are busy or the puppy needs some quiet time on his own, put him in his basket in a playpen. Give him some toys and cover the floor with newspaper in case of accidents.

Flooring

Until the puppy has learnt bladder control, its playpen will obviously have to stand on a washable floor when in the house. It is very important to clean the floor thoroughly when mopping up after accidents, in order to remove the puppy's own odour from the spot. The use of an odour-eliminating fluid may be helpful. If this is not done, the puppy will continue to urinate and defecate in the same place. Use sheets of newspaper to cover the floor; this will protect it and help in the house-training of small puppies (see page 26).

The puppy's bed

In the early days it is necessary to ensure that the puppy actually sleeps in its bed. Certainly for the first few nights a new puppy will be likely to try to stop you from leaving it alone. Do resist the temptation to let your puppy to sleep in your own room; it is bad training for the puppy and there is always the risk that fleas (which your puppy may have) will breed in your bedding (see page 38).

▲ A strong rubber kong toy filled with tasty treats will keep a puppy occupied and prevent boredom.

A very suitable puppy bed is illustrated below. Made of rigid plastic, it is available in a range of sizes and is relatively inexpensive, light, washable, waterproof, and reasonably resistant to the puppy's destructive skills. It is meant to be used with soft, disposable or washable bedding. The traditional dog basket made of woven willow is not suitable for most puppies which would simply unravel it. Neither are 'bean bag' beds or foam bags suitable. Most young puppies would chew these and would risk swallowing pieces of the filling.

Playthings

Most puppies derive great pleasure from a big marrow bone, but you should only offer a raw beef shin bone. It is a natural plaything, cleans the teeth, helps in the shedding of milk teeth, exercises the jaws and provides some calcium. Never give a puppy small bones that may break or splinter, and also beware of a puppy swallowing excessive amounts of powder-fine but indissoluble fragments from cooked bones. Dog chews are a good substitute and certainly less hazardous. As such, these may be given to puppies in preference to bones.

A wide variety of puppy toys is available. Choose with care and avoid those that mimic personal possessions, such as slippers, or it will hardly be surprising if the puppy makes the mistake of thinking all slippers are playthings.

▶ You should invest in a strong plastic basket which is difficult to destroy and line it with some soft towels or, better still, 'vet bed'.

An outdoor kennel

As household pets, most dogs are given a base in the home and take part in the life of the family. However, there may be practical reasons why this is not possible, especially with some of the larger, heavier-coated breeds or in the case of working dogs. Dogs are quite adaptable to life in a dry, well-insulated kennel and will, if necessary, grow a suitably thick, protective winter coat.

If you plan to house your puppy outside, buy it in spring or summer so that it has time to acclimatize as winter approaches. A dog kept outside will still identify with the family as its pack, and special care should be taken to give it plenty of human contact.

Kennel design

When choosing or designing a kennel, the three vital requirements are that it should be weatherproof, draughtproof and well-ventilated. It should be raised about 10 cm (4 in) off the ground to allow for ventilation underneath and to avoid damp penetration. The roof should be pitched to shed rain and snow, and the eaves should overhang sufficiently to carry water away from the walls.

As a protection against draughts, there should be a porch and the entrance should be at the front rather than at a gable end. The front (or, alternatively, the roof) should be hinged so that the kennel can be opened up for easy cleaning.

The eventual adult size of the dog should be borne in mind; a growing puppy will not mind having extra space, provided that its bed is snug, but an adult dog will be very unhappy in a kennel that is too small. As a general guide, the kennel should be big enough to allow the adult dog freedom of movement, and the door should be at least one-and-a-half times the width of the adult.

Essential kennel furniture consists of a good bed and some warm bedding. It goes without saying that this should be washed frequently and the kennel should be kept scrupulouly clean. The dog should have access to toys and chews to keep it occupied and prevent boredom.

Siting

Careful consideration should be given to the siting of the kennel. It should be placed so that the door is away from the prevailing wind and out of the heat of the midday sun. If possible, the site should allow the puppy to see the most frequently used house door and some of the activity going on around it. The fact that a puppy is kept outside and therefore has more freedom than one kept in the house should not be made an excuse to deny it accompanied exercise or the love and attention that every dog expects and is entitled to.

Choosing a puppy

The most important thing about selecting a puppy is to take plenty of time over it. Impulse purchases of puppies, as of other things, are often regretted.

Where to buy

Your local veterinary surgeon can advise you on reputable local breeders and other sources of supply. Alternatively, animal welfare organizations can often help. Many breed societies have 'rescue' associations offering puppies which have been abandoned or are not required for breeding purposes. Some of the latter may have minor defects of appearance which make them unsuitable for showing or breeding but do not affect their suitability as pets. An alternative source is a reputable animal home. Puppies should not be obtained from pet shops.

Whenever possible, see the puppy with its mother and siblings. Look for an active, healthy puppy (see page 35) and do not be tempted to choose the runt of the litter out of pity.

Documentation

Preferably, puppies should have received the first vaccinations in their immunization programme before they leave the dam (mother), and the vendor should supply an interim vaccination certificate. Purchase must be after, or conditional on, a satisfactory veterinary examination. Pedigree puppies should be accompanied by an official pedigree certificate and Kennel Club registration document. The other essential piece of documentation for the new owner is a diet sheet showing how the puppy has been fed so far. Moving to a new home is enough of an upset for a young puppy without adding to it by the stress of feeding unfamiliar food. Any desired changes from the former diet should be made gradually once the puppy has settled in.

In law, buying a puppy attracts the same statutory rights as any other purchase. Many good breeders also ask that if, at any time in the future, the dog cannot be kept, it should be returned to them.

▲ With these Yorkshire Terrier puppies, as with all other pedigree dogs, an official pedigree certificate and evidence of registration with The Kennel Club should be supplied by the vendor, and the purchase should be conditional upon veterinary clearance.

▼ When choosing a puppy at a breeder's house, you should always ask to see the mother to assess her temperament.

Introducing the new puppy

The change from the familiar comfort of its mother and siblings to the novel surroundings of a new home is bewildering and potentially frightening for a puppy, and every effort must be made to calm its fears and provide an orderly introduction to its new way of life. Important considerations, such as where the puppy's bed is to go, where its food and water bowls will be sited, and which parts of the house it is allowed access to, should have been decided in advance. The bed and bowls should already be in place, so that from the start the puppy can see that its essential needs have been provided for.

Children and pets

It is difficult to restrain young children from gathering round to admire a new puppy, but for the first day or two they should keep their distance and avoid noise and sudden movements. When the puppy feels sufficiently at ease in its new surroundings it will come forward of its own accord and indicate that it is ready to make friends. Very young children should not be left unsupervised with a puppy.

Use the puppy's name frequently from the beginning. After the settling-in period, it will be ready to start playing, but games must be

◀ Cats will usually stand their ground even when faced by an inquisitive puppy which is much larger than them. Indeed, size is no barrier to friendship, and cats are often more tolerant of large than small dogs.

gentle and should not go on for more than a few minutes at a session. If there are any other pets in the house, these must be introduced to the new arrival with care. Cats tend to treat new puppies with caution and may keep well out of their way for a few days while they assess the risks. Make sure that, in the excitement of the new arrival, older pets continue to receive their share of attention.

Temporary isolation

Until the first course of vaccinations has been completed, usually at about ten to twelve weeks, your puppy must not be allowed into areas where other, unvaccinated, dogs may have walked. This means that it must be confined to your own yard or garden, and must be carried if it ventures outside (for example, to visit the veterinary surgery).

▶ Introduce the new puppy to other family members but be sure to supervise children initially.

Feeding

The balanced diet

The essential constituents of a balanced diet for every puppy are protein, fat, carbohydrate, vitamins, minerals, water and roughage.
- **Protein** (meat, offal, fish and, occasionally, cheese and eggs) must account for a considerable proportion of the diet. Meat and fish that are fit for human consumption may be fed raw; offal should be cooked and fed only in moderation.
- **Carbohydrate** is obtained from such cereal foods as biscuit and biscuit meal, wholemeal bread and, for young puppies, puppy meal, cooked rice, baby cereals and porridge.
- **Fat** is obtained from the protein foods and from milk.
- **Extra vitamins and minerals** should be given to puppies in a calcium-rich mineral/vitamin supplement.
- **Roughage** is provided by cereal foods and vegetables. As dogs synthesize vitamin C, greens need not be given.
- **Fresh drinking water** must always be within reach.

Convenience foods

Some varieties of prepared canned foods contain a mixture of proteins and carbohydrates with supplements, and these brands are designed to meet all a puppy's nutritional needs. Others contain meat intended to be fed with cereal

▼ Puppies will need to be fed little and often; the number of meals can be reduced as they mature.

such as biscuit or biscuit meal. When additional cereal is indicated, feed an equal volume of cereal and tinned food.

Dried foods are also intended to provide all the dog's nutritional needs. However, they have the disadvantage of monotony and may create increased thirst in the puppy which must be satisfied by the provision of a generous supply of fresh drinking water. Some dried foods require the addition of water and a period of soaking before being given to the puppy to eat.

Whichever food you decide on, follow the manufacturer's advice about quantities and you must always allow for individual variation between puppies. Your veterinary surgeon will advise on feeding if any difficulties arise.

▲ Make sure that your dog always has fresh water to drink.

The puppy at two to four months

Whenever possible, follow the breeder's feeding notes while your new puppy is settling in, and make changes only gradually. A very young puppy needs food that is easy to digest, so minced meat (particularly white meat), flaked fish and cooked cereal foods are important constituents of its diet. At this age the puppy will need four regular meals a day: water and cereal at 8 am; meat and cereal at noon; water and cereal at 4 pm; and more meat and cereal at 8 pm Avoid feeding milk. Alternatively, you can provide a balanced diet that is designed specifically for puppies.

The puppy at four to ten months

As the puppy grows, the number of meals offered is reduced, whereas the amount of food offered at each meal is increased. At four months, you should omit one of the water and cereal meals; at six months, stop giving the other. By ten months, only the small breeds will need to be given two meals a day. The larger breeds will thrive on one main meal and one much smaller meal.

Vegetarian foods

Vegetarians and vegans sometimes wish to provide their dogs with a non-meat diet. Such foods are available, but they should be used only with veterinary advice. (Note: a cat's diet, however, must include protein of animal origin.)

▲ If in doubt about feeding bones to puppies, fibre or hide chews make a good substitute and will provide excellent exercise for teeth and gums.

Treats

Most puppies will try to beg titbits from the family but, however hard they are to resist, the sensible owner will take a firm line from the beginning. It is always difficult to restrain children from sharing their sweets and crisps with their family pet, but these are highly unsuitable foods,especially for puppies. Chocolate, in particular, is poisonous to dogs and puppies. There must be an absolute embargo on children feeding treats to the dog. Puppies can be discouraged by putting a protective hand over the desired item and saying firmly 'Mine!' However, it is always best to keep temptation out of the way by not eating treats in front of a puppy.

Similarly, from the beginning, puppies should be discouraged from begging at family mealtimes. It may be that there are small 'left-overs' which can be given as a treat, but this should take place after the family meal is over and should be fed in the dog's own bowl. However, this should be a special concession rather than a regular occurrence.

Titbits have an invaluable role to play in training your puppy, and a reward is sometimes appropriate at other times, too. Suitable items can be obtained at pet shops, although take care before you buy: some things sold as 'dog treats' can be unsuitable.

Exercise

Young puppies expend enormous amounts of energy in play, and between their periods of frantic activity should be left to sleep a great deal in a quiet place, undisturbed by children or the household routine.

Their only outdoor playground during the first three months of life is the garden, which must surely be a source of great pleasure to them after the restrictions imposed on them in the house. It may be near impossible to make a garden totally puppy-proof, but part of it must be enclosed if the puppy is to enjoy some play in the fresh air.

During these early months, puppies need to be kept away from other dogs, and even away from places where other dogs may have been, in order to minimize the risk of contracting disease by cross-infection before their own vaccination regime has had time to give them immunity (see page 36). This need for caution means that going out for even short walks is impossible before the puppy is at least twelve weeks old and is fully vaccinated.

◀ Put aside some time each day to play with your puppy in the garden. It will enjoy boisterous games with a toy or ball.

▶ Get your puppy used to wearing a soft collar from an early age. Attach a lead and just let it trail behind the puppy as it runs around the house.

Collars and leads

As the puppy matures, it will need to be accustomed to wearing a collar and being held on a lead. Try putting the collar on the puppy for short periods – perhaps before feeding, so that the pleasure of the meal will overcome the aversion to wearing a collar, until it is accepted without fuss. Next introduce the puppy to the lead; fix it on to the collar for short periods until the puppy becomes used to that, too. Only then can you attempt to take the puppy out in order to encourage it to walk on a lead.

Short-nosed puppies, such as Pekingeses and Pugs, will be safer and more comfortable in a harness. Long-necked breeds will be more comfortable in a broad collar. Avoid using chain collars on long-haired breeds which are better suited to rolled collars. Collars should be loose enough to allow two fingers to slip between the collar and the neck, and you should test the fit of your puppy's collar frequently. You will need to provide new collars as your puppy grows bigger and stronger.

How much exercise?

It soon becomes obvious just how much exercise is needed for the big, boisterous breeds, such as the Irish Setter, and for the strong, steady breeds, such as the Labrador Retriever. Increase an exercise programme gradually until, at maturity, the most energetic dogs are having perhaps 16 km (10 miles) a day, as well as plenty of freedom in an enclosed garden. About 1.5 km (1 mile) is probably enough for the smallest breeds.

Basic training and socialization

Puppies learn all about life at an early age, known as the socialization period, which lasts until about 12 weeks. During this time, they meet potentially frightening objects, such as washing machines and vacuum cleaners. If a puppy gets used to them by gentle introduction, it will accept them for the rest of its life. The same applies to meeting other animals. Accordingly, you should make a positive effort to get your puppy out and about as soon as it is safe to do so.

◀ A puppy must get used to walking on a lead. In towns, a lead will protect your puppy from traffic and keep it from places where young children play – dog faeces can be a hazard. In the countryside, always use a lead when walking near livestock.

House-training

This should begin in a quiet, unemphatic way as soon as the puppy is brought home. Puppies urinate frequently, and success in house-training depends on anticipating their needs. Regardless of weather, the puppy must be taken outside for a few moments every time it wakes up and after eating or drinking. Praise the puppy according to performance. This method is suitable for older and/or larger breeds of puppy.

Small breeds and very young puppies may be trained to urinate and defecate on newspapers spread on the floor. Praise when the papers are used. Gradually move the papers nearer to an outside door and then into the garden before discarding them altogether. Some puppies are house-trained quickly; others take three months or more to learn bladder control.

Simple commands

From an early age, you can teach your puppy certain commands, such as 'heel', 'sit', 'stay' and 'come'. You must take care to always use the same word, and it must sound distinct from all the other words. It is very important to be consistent in training, to teach only one command at a time, and not to over-estimate the puppy's span of concentration. Initially, only one person in the family should undertake the training so that the puppy is not confused. Later, when it is familiar with the basic commands, it will respond to them when given by others.

◀ Most dogs are highly receptive to training and eager to please. An untrained dog can be a danger to you, itself and the public.

Effective training is achieved by using rewards and punishment, in the form of praise and the withholding of rewards. Generous praise should be given for every success, even a belated one. Keep training sessions very short to begin with, and always ensure that the puppy wears a collar and lead so that you can control it.

Elementary obedience training classes are recommended as soon as the puppy can be admitted. Although elaborate training is usually inappropriate for pet dogs, a sensible measure of control is vital for safety and enjoyable companionship.

▶ Learning to sit, lie down, stay at heel or come when called; these and a few other simple commands will make life easier for you and your puppy.

▼ Teaching your puppy to stay. With the puppy in the sitting or lying position, raise your hand and give it the command 'stay'. Next, move slowly away a pace or two with your hand still raised. Try to keep your puppy's attention, maintaining eye contact with him all the time. After a short time, praise him and call him to you. Reward him with a titbit.

Household dangers

Puppies want to investigate the world in which they find themselves. This cannot and should not be discouraged, but it can lead them into danger. Before a new puppy is brought home, it is worth considering what hazards it will face around the house, and what precautions may be taken. Ordinary household items, such as pans of boiling water, hot fat, live cables, toxic cleaners, such as bleach, and tablets are all potential death-traps and, as such, must be kept well out of reach.

In the garden
A particular danger area is the garden, so before your puppy is allowed to run free outside, you should check for possible hazards and either remove them or put them behind secure fencing. Remove any ladders or other fixtures which give access to flat roofs or balconies. Garden ponds should be fenced off temporarily while the puppy is young. Never move your car until you know that the puppy is safely out of the way. Puppies are sometimes excited by car movements, and it is best to restrain them or put them indoors. Always check, before shutting the garage that the puppy is not inside.

Gates
These must close securely and should be constructed in such a way that a puppy cannot wriggle through them. Plastic garden fencing stapled to the gate framework makes a good barrier which can be removed when the puppy is too large to clamber through. Make sure

▶ Puppies are naturally curious and investigate and play with all sorts of unlikely items. Don't leave things that they can damage or which could harm them lying around.

that your children understand the importance of closing the gate at all times, and urge this on regular visitors, too. Fixing a postbox to the gate on the outside reduces the need for deliveries to the door.

Fences and hedges
Check that these are puppy-proof. Remember that some breeds, especially terriers, are instinctive diggers and it is possible for a puppy to dig its way out of a garden. Plastic garden fencing can be used to block up gaps, fixing it in place with garden canes. Sinking it about 15 cm (6 in) into the ground will discourage burrowing. Alternatively, bricks or blocks may be placed against it.

Equipment
The electric flexes of garden equipment look like tempting playthings to a puppy. Confine your dog to a run or to the house while garden equipment is in use. This also applies to mowers, hedge-trimmers and similar items. Ensure that pesticides and other garden chemicals are stored out of reach, and that they are kept out of the puppy's way when in use. Before using such products, check that they are safe for animals; if in doubt, ask your veterinary surgeon.

▲ Many dogs love to dig – to bury bones and other objects or to escape. Make your garden escape-proof and protect your plants from enthusiastic diggers.

◀ If you have a workshop or garden shed, be sure to keep all toxic chemicals and sharp tools locked up or well out of your puppy's way.

Grooming

Grooming is always necessary, and not just for good looks. It removes debris, such as dust, dead skin, loose hairs and burrs; prevents serious tangling and matting; massages the skin and improves muscle tone; reveals parasites and other problems; and gives the puppy a sense of wellbeing and belonging to the new family or pack.

The amount of grooming needed by any particular puppy will depend on its coat type, but some daily attention should be given to all puppies to accustom them to being handled and examined. Those puppies, usually long haired, that will need extensive grooming throughout life must learn to accept it as part of their daily routine.

Long-haired puppies

Many people find long-haired puppies particularly attractive. There are many mongrels and cross-breds with long coats as well as pedigree puppies, such as the Chow Chow, Rough Collie, Setters, Maltese, Old English Sheepdog, Afghan Hound, Pekingese, Pomeranian, Golden Retriever, Shetland Sheepdog, Shih Tzu and Yorkshire Terrier.

Brushing, combing and stripping

If a long coat is to be kept in top condition, it is obligatory to brush and comb it daily to remove the loose hair. Another advantage of daily grooming is that carpets and household furnishings are kept relatively free of puppy hair. Unless preparing for the show bench (when special grooming

Grooming equipment

- Soft brush and bristle brush
- Wide- and fine-toothed combs
- Stripping comb
- Sharp scissors
- Rubber slicker
- Nail clippers

▶ Get your puppy used to being groomed and handled from an early age so that he will enjoy the contact with you and will not mind being groomed when adult.

▲ When grooming your puppy, don't forget to brush him underneath on his belly (above left) and also around the anal area under his tail. Brush his coat firmly but gently to remove any dead hairs (above right).

▶ Finish the session by brushing vigorously; it should be pleasant for both of you. With a comb, gently tease out any matted hair and tangles in the long fur on his head (below right), ears, limbs and tail feathering.

techniques may be used), brush and comb in the direction the fur grows, and pay particular attention to the feathering on the limbs and tail.

In more natural conditions, the coat thickens up for the winter and moults for the summer. One major factor nowadays is that in centrally heated houses most puppies are kept too warm and, as a result, moult throughout the year. A saw-toothed stripping comb will help remove any loose hairs, and stripping is particularly desirable in the summer months when heavy-coated breeds may suffer from excessive heat.

Short- and wire-haired breeds

Short-haired breeds, such as the Boxer, Dalmatian, Greyhound, Pug and Whippet, may be brushed or groomed with a rough mitt. The wire-haired terrier breeds, including the Airedale, Fox, Scottish, Sealyham and West Highland White Terriers, need grooming with a very stiff brush and a metal comb. Daily grooming is desirable, even if brief. Many terriers also benefit from being stripped in summer.

▶ You can remove dead hairs in a terrier's coat by hand-stripping. Just take a few hairs between your thumb and forefinger and pull them out gently. It won't hurt (right). Use a rubber slicker or hound glove for grooming smooth-coated terriers and hounds (far right).

Bathing

Bathing is not usually recommended for puppies under six months of age. If necessary, in unusual circumstances, you can use a proprietary dog shampoo and rinse off each application thoroughly. Towel dry thoroughly and then finish drying the coat with a hairdryer.

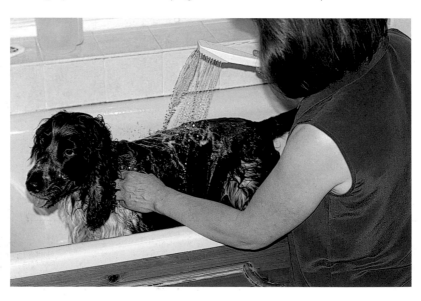

Clipping and trimming

Some puppies, such as Poodles and some terrier breeds, need clipping and they should be taken to a pet beauty parlour for professional attention, at least in the early months. Some owners will become adept at giving their pet a simple trim after they have seen it demonstrated a few times. Owners of long-haired puppies should use scissors to trim the hair between the digits to prevent it becoming uncomfortably matted, and also around the anus to prevent any matting due to dried faeces.

Nail-clipping (see page 13) is not advisable for very young puppies, but it may become necessary as they mature. Regular walking on roads or pavements will help to keep your puppy's nails in trim.

Inspection

Regular grooming sessions also provide an ideal opportunity to check on your puppy's general condition. See that the ears are clean, with no signs of discharge or debris, such as plant burrs. The eyes and nose should be clear and free of discharge. Check the paws for any grit or thorns between the pads, and the genital area for any unusual discharges. If you do notice something unusual, then consult your veterinary surgeon.

Oral hygiene

All puppies will benefit from being accustomed to having their teeth cleaned with water and a toothbrush from an early age. Regular cleaning helps prevent the build-up of plaque and, when they are a little older, tartar. If tartar deposits accumulate, the result will be receding gums, loosened teeth and very bad breath. Puppies most at risk are those of the short-faced and toy breeds which have overcrowded teeth.

▶ Clean your dog's teeth regularly with a toothpaste and water.

The healthy puppy

Puppies are generally resilient, happy and inquisitive, displaying the signs of health that are listed opposite. When they deviate from these, you should seek veterinary advice. You can do this initially, perhaps, by telephone. Most veterinary surgeons prefer to see prevaccinated puppies by appointment, partly to allow time to discuss such matters as feeding and general care but also so as not to endanger the puppy by putting it in close proximity to other animals which may carry disease.

Specific symptoms apart, the sign that a puppy is not well is often a change in its behaviour, such as lack of interest in its food or in a favourite game or toy, excessive sleepiness, over-excitement or even irritability. To detect these early warning signs of trouble, you should know your puppy well from regular observation.

Isolated vomiting need be no cause for concern provided that there are no other symptoms of illness – a change in diet may well be the reason. An older puppy will often eat grass to induce vomiting if it is feeling uncomfortable.

Examine your puppy regularly to check for tell-tale warnings of health problems. Look in his mouth, ears and nose for any discharge and wipe carefully with a damp cloth. Check the coat for fleas – they will look like specks of coal dust in the fur.

Signs of health

Abdomen	It should be rounded, not bulging; soft and flexible, not taut or drum-like; not potbellied; no swelling around the navel.
Anus	It should be clean, with no staining, scouring, or matting by dry faeces; it is normal for puppies to sniff under tails to identify other dogs by anal scent.
Appetite	The puppy should be enthusiastic for food; no undue scavenging; no vomiting.
Breathing	It should be quiet and even when at rest; no laboured breathing; no coughing; normally panting to cool down.
Claws	There should be no splitting; no overgrown claws.
Coat	It should be clean, pleasant-smelling; free from parasites, loose hairs and dirt; soft to the touch, not staring or brittle.
Demeanour	The puppy should be curious, alert, vital; quickly responsive to sounds and calls.
Ears	Alert to slightest sound; clean, with no brown or yellow deposits; head and ears held in normal position; no scratching, rubbing or shaking of the head.
Eyes	They should be clear, with no cloudiness of the cornea; not unduly sensitive to light; no discharge or weeping; not bloodshot.
Faeces	These should be consistently formed; colour varying according to diet; should be passed regularly two to four times daily.
Movement	This tends to be very active in short spurts with rest periods between; young puppies may sleep 16 out of 24 hours; gambolling, unco-ordinated movement normal; young puppies tend to fall over their own feet; no limping or lameness.
Nose	Its condition depends on the environment; likely to be cold and damp out of doors, warm and dry indoors; no persistent discharge; nostrils not blocked by dried mucus.
Pads	There should be no matting of hair between the digits due to contamination by mud, tar or grease; no cracked pads.
Skin	Loose and supple; clean, without scurf, inflammation, parasites, or sores.
Teeth	Clean and white; gums pink except those of the Chow which may show darker pigmentation; shedding of the milk teeth normal (see page 13).
Urine	This should be straw-coloured, not cloudy; no blood in the urine; passes urine frequently, with no difficulty; both sexes tend to squat to urinate until puberty, when the male begins to 'cock his leg'.

Vaccinations

Vaccination provides a puppy with protection against certain diseases, so it is important that all puppies should be vaccinated before they start going out for walks or mixing with other dogs.

The vendor of any puppy should give the new owner written details of any vaccinations. As soon as you get your puppy, ask your veterinary surgeon about completion of the programme and when booster injections will be required.

The record of your dog's vaccinations should be kept carefully and produced so that the veterinary surgeon can keep it up to date. No reputable boarding kennels will accept a dog that has not had a full programme of vaccinations.

Infectious canine diseases

Vaccination usually gives protection against seven serious and relatively common diseases (or disease fractions). These are canine distemper (including hardpad), viral hepatitis, parvovirus, two forms of leptospirosis and both parainfluenza virus and bordatella bronchiseptica (each a fraction of the kennel cough complex).

Fortunately, it is possible to obtain vaccines that may be used against a combination of diseases simultaneously. Vaccination is very safe and rarely causes an allergic reaction, although the puppy may feel a little drowsy.

Why vaccinate?

The purpose of vaccination is to stimulate the production of the puppy's own antibodies to combat the various disease organisms. This is achieved either by introducing a vaccine of dead disease organisms which cannot produce the disease but will activate the production of antibodies, or by introducing a live vaccine prepared from a weakened strain of the disease (or a strain that attacks other animals) and which is no threat to the puppy. Again, the result will be the production of the puppy's own antibodies. In countries where rabies is endemic, puppies will also need protection against this most dreaded of diseases; indeed, vaccination may be mandatory. At present the UK is free of rabies.

The vaccination regime

Most vaccines (but not all) are administered by subcutaneous injection. The usual procedure is for the puppy to receive two injections at an interval of two to four weeks. The first of these is given at between eight and twelve weeks of age, according to the risk factors.

Most young puppies from a reliable source will receive some immunity from their mother, by way of antibodies in her milk. When the first injection has to be given early, the presence of these maternal antibodies can interfere with the effectiveness of the vaccination. Any regime, therefore, may need adjusting to suit the needs of an individual puppy. For this reason, you should always seek advice from a veterinary surgeon as to the exact timing of the injections as soon as you acquire the puppy.

Vaccines do not give life-long protection and all need boosting at regular intervals: some at six months; some after one or two years. Without boosters the degree of protection can fall dangerously low.

▲ The puppy's early visits to the veterinary surgeon can help pave the way for a good relationship.

▼ Get your puppy used to being handled from an early age. Always take him to the vet on a lead and hold him firmly while he is examined.

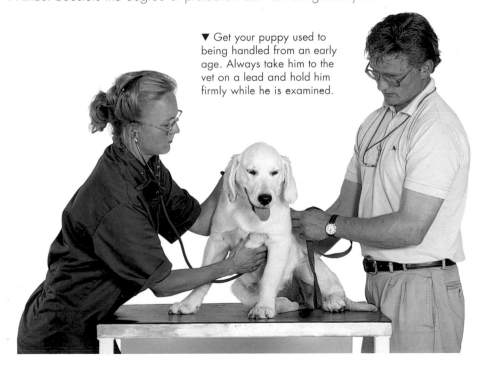

Ailments and parasites

Diarrhoea

This is a very common complaint in puppies. Diarrhoea may be due to the puppy having eaten unfamiliar or unsuitable food, or to an infection caused by bacteria or parasites. It may, on rare occasions, be caused by an obstruction in the intestine as a result of the puppy having swallowed a stone, marble or some other foreign body. If it persists, or is accompanied by vomiting, you must seek veterinary advice. It may be a symptom of disease and produce rapid debilitation or even death through dehydration.

Motion sickness

When travelling by car, a high proportion of puppies are affected by motion sickness, with symptoms of nausea, panting and vomiting. The anxiety can also cause diarrhoea. Tranquillizing and anti-motion sickness drugs may be prescribed while the puppy remains prone to such sickness, but most become accustomed to car travel. As soon as the early vaccinations are complete, it helps to take your puppy out in the car twice a day between meal times just for a few minutes at a time.

Ear mites

A puppy that scratches or rubs its ears, or shakes its head, may have an infestation of ear mites. These parasites feed on the delicate lining of the ear by piercing through the skin. Serum seeps from the wounds to make a characteristic deposit in the ear canal which, in extreme cases, can become completely blocked.

Ear mites can cause intense suffering to a puppy, yet control can be achieved if a prompt veterinary diagnosis is obtained. In neglected cases, the ear drum may be pierced, and permanent middle ear damage can result with such symptoms as loss of balance and convulsions. If your puppy displays any of the symptoms listed above, take it to the vet as soon as possible.

▲ You should examine your puppy's ears regularly to check for inflammation. Excess hair inside the ears can harbour mites and may need plucking.

Fleas

A puppy that scratches itself furiously may be found to have fleas crawling and occasionally jumping through its fur. These reddish-brown parasites feed by piercing the puppy's skin with their mouthparts and sucking on its blood. Flea droppings, which on examination will be seen in the puppy's coat, are in fact the dark colour of dried blood, containing whole blood cells. There will also be minute clots of blood in the fur, formed when the wounds continue to bleed. The puncture wounds can become infected, dermatitis may occur, and the flea (as an intermediate host) may transmit tapeworms.

Infestation is most likely in warm weather when the life cycle of the flea may be as short as 30 days. It is not enough merely to eliminate an infestation from the puppy's coat. Control is only successful when it destroys the fleas in their breeding places, notably the puppy's bed and bedding and their surroundings, so be sure to treat these, too. Check any other pets for fleas, too. Veterinary advice should be taken both on the treatment of the infestation and future prevention. Preparations include sprays, shampoos and powders. After the fleas have been eradicated, you should continue to check your puppy's coat for the after-effects mentioned above.

▲ When using flea spray, remove and spray the puppy's collar before spraying him. Protect the puppy's eyes and mouth.

Lice

An infestation of lice will also make a puppy scratch furiously and frequently. Two species of biting lice and one sucking louse may attack the puppy. The biting lice cannot pierce the skin but cluster in great numbers around abrasions and at body openings to feed on the natural secretions. Sucking lice pierce the skin to feed. In long-coated puppies it is not easy to see the lice. They are small, dull and rather transparent, and tend to cling to the skin. The white nits, or eggs, however, show up well, particularly on a dark coat.

Puppies suffer great discomfort from lice: the sores caused by scratching may become infected; anaemia may be caused by sucking lice; and biting lice (as intermediate hosts) may transmit tapeworms.

The nits hatch in seven to ten days, and the young are mature at about 14 days. Once fertilized, the female lice lay several eggs a day for their entire life of about 30 days. Veterinary help should be sought if you suspect that your puppy has lice.

▲ Combing your puppy's coat with a special flea comb will soon reveal whether there are any fleas present.

Worms

In severe cases, roundworms will be seen in the puppy's faeces, or may be vomited, but even without symptoms, all puppies need to be treated for roundworm infestation. Normally a puppy acquired at eight weeks of age will have been wormed several times by the breeder. It is essential, however, that further worming takes place. Do not attempt home cures but consult your veterinary surgeon about this when you are arranging for the puppy's first vaccination.

Dogs should be wormed about once every four months to reduce the risk of passing worm eggs which can lead to serious infection (toxocariasis) in children.

▲ Some flea applications are applied directly to the skin behind the puppy's head. These are particularly effective.

Handling a sick dog

From time to time, your puppy may suffer from some kind of ailment, either mild or serious. In these situations it is necessary to take some action. Some of the essential nursing techniques are outlined below.

◀ Holding the muzzle: it is often necessary to hold a puppy's muzzle while it is being treated. The hand should be closed lightly but firmly over the muzzle, with the thumb on top and the fingers below.

▲ Tablets: the top jaw is opened gently with one hand and the lower jaw with the other, leaving thumb and forefinger free to place the tablet well back on the tongue. Hold the muzzle closed and stroke the throat to assist swallowing.

◀ Lifting and weighing a puppy: you should always support a puppy with one hand under his rear and the other around his chest when lifting him. Some puppies can be weighed on the kitchen scales. Alternatively, stand with the puppy in your arms on the bathroom scales and then subtract your weight from the scale reading.

First aid

The aims of first aid for puppies should always be to:
- Limit the animal's suffering or injury.
- Prevent further injury.
- Keep the puppy as quiet and comfortable as possible.
- Seek veterinary help urgently.

Injuries
The veterinary surgeon, if telephoned and given details of the problem, will advise whether the puppy should be brought to the surgery or should wait to be seen on the spot. Sometimes, as in a road accident, moving him may be unavoidable. An injured puppy should be lifted using both arms so that support is distributed evenly. If a fracture is suspected, he should be carried and laid down with the damaged limb uppermost.

Cleansing wounds
Pending veterinary attention, major bleeding should be stopped or stemmed by placing a clean handkerchief on the wound. Less major wounds may be bathed in a mild saline solution: 1 teaspoon of salt to 500 ml (1 pint) water). Don't use disinfectants or commercial antiseptics.

Shock
Shock may result from electrocution, wasp or bee stings, burns, poisoning or a heart attack. The puppy should be kept warm and, if necessary, the heart should be massaged gently. Seek veterinary help immediately.

Heat exhaustion
Puppies and dogs are prone to heat exhaustion which may result in complete collapse, coma and even death. Puppies that become overheated may be sprinkled with a garden spray or shower attachment to cool them down. They should not be plunged into a cold bath as this may be too much of a shock to their systems. If you suspect heat stroke, then obtain veterinary attention at once.

Under no circumstances should dogs ever be left alone in parked cars, caravans, canvas tents or cabin cruisers in warm weather.

▲ A puppy with suspected heat exhaustion should be hosed down with plenty of cold water immediately. You may also need ice packs.

Dogs and the law

Dog registration

Stray dogs cause many problems in the community – dog fouling, road accidents and attacks on people and animals. The old licence was abolished in 1988 but the RSPCA believes that a compulsory national registration scheme with the permanent identification of dogs (through an identichip implant or tattooing, in addition to the existing collar tag) must be introduced to encourage responsible ownership. The revenue raised from registration fees would go towards a network of dog wardens who would pick up stray dogs and attempt to reunite them with their owners and administer the law against irresponsible owners.

Dogs worrying livestock

The owner or person in charge of a dog found to be worrying livestock (cattle, sheep, goats, pigs, horses, asses, mules and poultry) is likely to be prosecuted and also to be held liable for heavy damages. The dog may also be made the subject of a control or destruction order. A farmer who shoots a dog in these circumstances is legally in a strong position.

Dangerous dogs

If a magistrates' court, upon complaint, considers that a dog is dangerous and not properly controlled, even if on the owner's property, it may make an order requiring the owner to control the dog, or, alternatively, it may order the dog to be destroyed and can appoint a person to carry out the destruction. In addition, the owner may be disqualified from having custody of a dog for a certain period. Substantial penalties may be imposed for breach of such an order or for failure to hand over a dog for destruction.

Dogs involved in accidents

Any driver involved in a road accident with a dog must stop. It is an offence to drive on, knowingly leaving the dog to suffer. The accident

Suspected cruelty cases

If you suspect that a dog is being subjected to cruelty, ask the RSPCA to investigate the case in confidence. Please ring the RSPCA 24-hour national cruelty and advice line – 0870 55 55 999.

must be reported to the police. The owner of a dog judged to have caused an accident may be liable to third party claims for damage. You should take out suitable insurance cover against such a contingency.

Dog collars

It is compulsory for a dog to wear a collar, bearing the owner's name and address, when in a public place. This applies to all pet dogs, but some dogs, such as packs of hounds and working sheepdogs, are exempt. The RSPCA also recommends that all dogs are microchipped.

Dogs and nuisance

Local authorities in the UK have the power to designate certain roads in which dogs must not only wear a collar and identification, but must also be kept on a lead. There may also be bylaws that provide penalties for owners or keepers of dogs that foul public places or which, by repeated barking, cause a nuisance to local residents.

Travel to and from the UK

The Pet Travel Scheme allows dogs travelling from western European countries and some other destinations to return to the UK without quarantine, as long as they meet certain conditions. Your vet will tell you what you need to do to get your pet protected against rabies, identified with a microchip and certified so it can travel with you. Travelling abroad can be hazardous in hot weather, particularly in cars or on ferries, so it may be better to leave your dog in kennels at home.

Insurance

As an owner, you must expect to pay for routine veterinary treatment and should allow for the cost of this when deciding whether to take on the responsibility for a puppy. You can insure for unexpected veterinary expenses and any legal claim for damages caused by a puppy, as in a road accident. We strongly recommend you take out insurance.

For a modest annual premium, a typical policy provides cover for the cost of treatment for accident, injury or illness, with certain exceptions, such as vaccinations and neutering. It also covers legal liability, including legal costs, third party injury or damage to property. Supplementary premiums cover loss, theft, or accidental death of a pet.

Your questions answered

My children think it unfair that if they are given sweets our puppy mustn't have any. Am I right to make this a strict rule?

Certainly. Sweets damage puppies' teeth at the vital growth stage and can cause obesity and heart conditions later in life. Puppies should not be encouraged to expect 'treats' between meals. Rewards given in training are another matter, but these should be chosen carefully. Many 'dog treats' sold by pet shops contain sugar and are highly unsuitable. Some owners keep a jar of small pieces of wholemeal bread baked hard in the oven and cut into cubes like croutons. Other suitable rewards include small pieces of charcoal biscuit or, occasionally, fragments of cheese. Remember that rewards lose their value if offered routinely. They should be given only in recognition of specific achievements.

We would like a puppy but we are all out during the day. Can you recommend a breed that could be left in the house during school and working hours?

No. No dog should be left on its own all day. Dogs are pack animals, and for the domesticated dog its owner's family takes the place of the pack. To deprive a dog of human company for long periods causes stress and will almost certainly lead to damage to furniture and furnishings as the dog becomes bored. A dog left alone may also create a noise nuisance to neighbours.

We are planning our holiday. How young can puppies be left in boarding kennels?

Reputable boarding kennels will not accept puppies that have not completed their initial course of injections, which means an effective minimum of about four months. Always inspect the kennels first. It is a good idea to arrange for a one- or two-night 'induction course' for the puppy's first experience of kennels. This will help it to adjust to a longer stay when you go on holiday.

My puppy occasionally picks up ticks on walks. What is the best way to deal with them?

Do not try to comb or pull the tick out. This will leave its head still buried in the puppy's skin. Use a tick-removing tool which can be bought from a pet shop or your vet.

I have seen an advertisement for local obedience classes. Do you recommend these for my puppy?

Most owners are able to cope with general obedience training themselves. The essentials are regular short daily sessions, with the accent on lavish praise for achievement. However, if you are a first-time dog owner a class will give you the basic ground rules and additional confidence and will help to socialize the puppy with other dogs. Basic training (see pages 26–7) is essential, but there is little point in subjecting your puppy to elaborate routines, which may give more satisfaction to you, the owner, than to the dog.

Is it safe to feed my puppy bones?

A bone gives a puppy great pleasure and helps the teeth to form properly. But it must be uncooked, large and without splintered ends. Never give chop, chicken or game bones. Rawhide dog chews from pet shops are a safe and acceptable alternative.

When should we buy a collar and tag for our new puppy?

There are two reasons for providing a dog with a collar and identity tag. One is so that it carries a means of identification (and this is a legal requirement in some countries including Britain). The other is that, without a collar and lead any kind of training is virtually impossible. Puppies are prone to stray and lose their way, and it is recommended that you fit a light puppy collar from the start. The RSPCA also recommends that your pet is microchipped – ask your veterinary surgeon for further details.

Life history

Scientific name	*Canis familiaris*
Gestation period	63 days (approx.)
Litter size	1–6 (small breeds) 5–12 (large breeds)
Birth weight	100 g ($3^1/_2$ oz) – 500 g (1 lb 2 oz)
Eyes open	10 days
Weaning age	35–49 days
Puberty	males 8–12 months females 6–18 months (commonly 8 months)
Adult weight	1 kg (2 lb 4 oz) – 70 kg (150 lb)
Best age to breed	males 350+ days females 540+ days
Oestrus (or season)	2 seasons per year
Duration of oestrus	3 weeks
Retire from breeding	males 8 years
	females 6–8 years
Life expectancy	10–18 years (small dogs usually outlive larger breeds)

Index

Why not learn more about other popular pets with further titles from the bestselling RSPCA Pet Guide series?

PET GUIDE

€ Collins Care for your
Kitten

0-00-718271-6

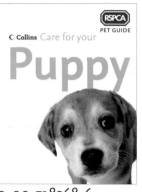

€ Collins Care for your
Puppy

0-00-718268-6

€ Collins Care for your
Rabbit

0-00-718270-8

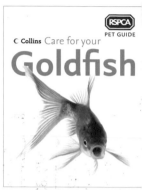

€ Collins Care for your
Goldfish

0-00-718272-4

€ Collins Care for your
Guinea Pig

0-00-718269-4

€ Collins Care for your
Budgerigar

0-00-719358-0

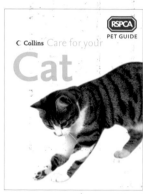

€ Collins Care for your
Cat

0-00-719356-4

Paperback
£4.99   48pp

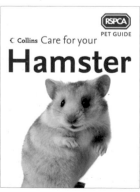

€ Collins Care for your
Hamster

0-00-719357-2

€ Collins Care for your
Tropical Fish

0-00-719359-9

To order any of these titles, please telephone **0870 787 1732**
For further information about all Collins books, visit our website: **www.collins.co.uk**